THE FLEECING OF AMERICA'S BABY BOOMERS

Is It That Your Advisor Doesn't Know or They Just Don't Care?

RICHARD D. LAFARGUE
EDITED BY DENISE BEATTY

Copyright © 2011 Richard D. LaFargue
- AR Ins. Lic. # 17515
All Rights Reserved.

ISBN: 146371467X
ISBN-13: 978-1463714673
LCCN: 2011912061

Securities offered through LaFargue Financial Group, Inc. a Registered Investment Advisor

CONTENTS

Chapter 1 The Financial Path 1

Chapter 2 Phases of Your Financial Life 7

Chapter 3 How Did We Get Into This Mess? 15

Chapter 4 What Can YOU Control? 21

Chapter 5 The Age 100 Rules 33

Chapter 6 Dollars-vs-Percentages 37

Chapter 7 Behavioral Economics 41

Chapter 8 Income Planning 47

Chapter 9 Secrets Revealed 49

Until We Meet Again 57

INTRODUCTION

It happens every day, not only in this country, but around the world. People blindly invest their money and have no idea exactly what their money is invested in. Their hope is that whatever investment the broker, or banker, sold them will be successful..... That such an investment will provide them with a secure and comfortable retirement... ...... It's sad to say that in most cases this is not the result that's achieved. In fact - their *chance* of success is just that....... a CHANCE!

The average investor in America has the deck stacked against them. It is virtually impossible for them to be consistently successful investing for their retirement unless they are aware of all the pitfalls that lie in their path. If you do not pay close attention to each and every detail, your plans will quickly become derailed, thus robbing you of your retirement dream. When it comes to financing your future, what you don't know can and will hurt you!

The problem lies with finding the right advisor. A simple feat..... right? ... Just because an annuity worked for the Smith's doesn't necessarily mean an annuity is the right answer for you. The Jones' IRA was their golden ticket, but are you in the same financial place for it to be yours as well? Flo at the beauty parlor said her advisor told her to put her money into gold! –Sound familiar??- Banter at the beauty shop and cookie cutter advisors shouldn't be your only option. Most people do not get good advice. The majority of future retirees don't fully understand what they own, or how it fits into a comprehensive approach to reaching their goals. This book was written in hopes of stimulating your interest in educating yourself about the things you can control while helping yourself achieve a secure and successful retirement.

I wrote this book to help **YOU**!

Sincerely,

Richard LaFargue

CHAPTER 1:
THE FINANCIAL PATH

"A journey of a thousand miles begins with a single step."
Lao-tzu, *The Way of Lao-tzu*
Chinese philosopher (604 BC - 531 BC)

Each and every one of us is on a Financial Path of some sort. Is it necessarily the path we want to be on? OR, perhaps we *think* our path is leading us to our perfect predetermined destination, when in reality we will end up in a less desirable location altogether!

To help better understand where *you* are, I have a few general questions for you to think about. Be brutally honest with yourself. Take time to reflect upon each question *and* each of your answers.

Do you feel you are on the right path to reach your financial goals for a successful retirement? Are you getting the financial results that you hoped to accomplish within your retirement portfolio? Have you sat down and analyzed how your cost of living will change after you officially begin retirement? Do you fully comprehend how losing a percentage of your salary (and/or health benefits) will impact your current lifestyle? Are you financially prepared for an increase in medical and prescription costs as you enter the Golden Years? Do you even have a retirement portfolio at this stage? Do you have any doubts that you will achieve your financial and personal goals? Is there uneasiness or feeling you have that is kind of eating away at you that you just haven't addressed? If you are already retired, do you have concerns that you may not have planned accordingly? Hhhmmm.... Are you *certain* that you're on the right path to achieve your goals?   If you're not on the right path, how do you get on the right path?

OK. Whew! How do you feel? Did your answers make you feel confident ..... or stressed? Are you satisfied with yourself and your financial future .... or more concerned than when you picked up this book?
Now that you've asked yourself a few of the tough questions and got an honest answer as to what your financial picture looks like, you're ready to take the first steps in that journey to making sure you are on the right path and that you have the right plan.
If we draw the analogy that achieving a successful retirement is like climbing Mount Everest, we may better realize completing such a feat will not be easy. There is a myriad of obstacles and conditions to overcome. You will need to spend a lot of time, energy and resources in planning the climb before you even set foot at the base. You'll be certain to have your double lined plastic boots, gaiters and crampons, rappel device, and many other tools necessary to complete the trek up and down the mountain. You'd even double check and TRIPLE check that you have the right equipment and supplies and most likely confer with a few experts before, during and after such a feat. Just like retirement planning! You too will complete research by utilizing the ideal resources and investment tools. You'll confirm and re-confirm that the IRA and annuity you have chosen are the perfect fit. You'll turn to your chosen expert for guidance and assistance throughout the various stages of your financial adventure.
Once you do get to the top – to retirement-- I'm certain you'll feel like shouting, "Yes, I've made it!" while feeling both exhilarated and peaceful in the same moment...... Just like those who reached the actual summit of Mount Everest and got to feel a great sense of accomplishment overcoming all the adversity and obstacles in their path.

The Financial Path

Aaahhh... You can breathe easy now!.... Right?? The view from such a vantage point can give clarity to your life. After all the planning and forethought, after all the research and self-doubt, now it's time to enjoy the days of no longer being at some company's beck and call... go golfing when the weather's warm, stay in bed when the snow falls..... sounds perfect! .... Not so fast! Are you aware that there are more people who die on the descent from Mount Everest, on the way down the mountain, than perish on the way up to the summit? That's right, more people die on the way down than on the way up. They are so joyous they have reached their ultimate goal that they let their judgments relax... they let their guard down. After all, they believe the hard part is over! That's where the biggest mistakes can lie! You see, just because you get to retirement doesn't mean that you are financially safe. There are more obstacles to consider.

Have you given thought to the fact that people are living a lot longer? Medical advances are capable of saving a heart attack or stroke victim. There are now many different methods to manage cancer. Broken hips and bad knees are becoming outpatient surgeries. Because of these scientific triumphs, today's average life expectancy is in upwards of 85 to 88 years.[1] One of the fastest-growing demographics in our society is the centurions, people who are at least 100 years old. Actually, the United States has the greatest number of centurions in the world at 70,490 as of September 1, 2010.[2] Did you create room in your financial plan for living to such an age? Did you consider the possibility of paying hundreds of dollars per month for prescriptions, or thousands each month for nursing home care?

---

1 http://www.cdc.gov/nchs/fastats/lifexpec.htm FASTSTATS Life Expectancy Table
2 Wikipedia.com September 1, 2010

You see, just getting to retirement is not good enough. There's a lot of living to do afterwards. Are you financially prepared for a long, successful retirement? Are you sure your plan will work? Are you excited about your future? If you cannot answer these questions with a resounding "YES!" you need to revamp your strategy. In the next few chapters we're going to look at some of the stumbling blocks that can keep you from achieving your financial goals. These obstacles are not always apparent. Some are hidden, while some are just mindlessly overlooked. Some of the problems are the result of you working with the wrong person to help you achieve your goals. Sometimes (get ready for this) you even *pay* for bad advice. Hard to believe, isn't it?

Have you ever been white water rafting? If you've had this experience, you know, they don't just put you in a raft and send you down the river; you have to at least be equipped with protective gear and learn a few basic commands as how to maneuver the raft. Let's paint the picture. You're in your raft, and you're drifting down the river. The sun is shining, with a light breeze blowing; it's just a gorgeous day. You might be thinking to yourself in this peaceful moment, why do we have on all this protective gear and why are we paying this guy sitting in the back of the raft so much money? This rafting stuff seems pretty simple.

In the next second, you round the bend and are suddenly dropped into class III rapids! This is where it gets a bit intimidating. The waves become larger and crest more rapidly causing your raft to pitch suddenly. The rocks jut out from the riverbed to create narrow, difficult passages that require expert maneuvering skills. This is when you grit your teeth and wonder why the heck you let your best friend talk you into such a vacation..... I mean, who chooses a vacation that could include returning with a few cracked ribs instead of a suntan and sand in your shoes?!?! ..... At this point, who do you think is the most important guy in the raft? If you said "the guide", you're absolutely right! When chaotic situations arise, you quickly realize how important protective gear is to you, and why you should follow your guide's instructions.

What's the connection to your retirement plan you ask? The part of "the guide" – the one who warns you of the possibilities of rough waters and ominous rocks – is your financial advisor....someone like me! I've been down the "river" and know the perils that lie ahead. I realize that your financial situation is significant to **you.** I understand that if you fall out of the raft and crack a few ribs, there are loved ones at home who will suffer if you did not plan financially for a medical disaster. I get that in life you want to take a few more vacations, travel to see your granddaughter's recital, or pay for your spouse's medical care when the insurance company denies coverage. I also know about the myths of financial planning that are widely accepted as truth. You see, I'm going to help you navigate your way through rough waters and help you achieve success.

This is where you ask yourself "Is my advisor being a good guide? Is he/she protecting me from all the hazards that lie in my pathway to success? Is the person I have entrusted with my financial future "scouting ahead" for the dangerous rocks or simply reacting to them when my raft slams against them? My question to you is: Are you paying for bad advice?

Is it that your advisor doesn't know or they just don't care?

CHAPTER 2:
PHASES OF YOUR FINANCIAL LIFE

Have you ever overheard parents speaking about their young children and their unruly behavior? One of the explanations you may hear the parents give for their child's actions is that they are just going through a phase. Our lives are defined by different phases that we pass through. The same is true with our financial lives.

Everyone's financial life can be broken down into three phases: the *accumulation phase*, the *preservation phase*, and the *distribution phase*. Let's take a close look at each phase and why it is important to understand how each segment is different. I believe understanding the financial phases of your life and how your money should be invested differently in each segment is critical to achieving success in your retirement! I want to give you a mental picture of this, so let's use the image of a tape measure.

Let's say we take a tape measure and stretch it out. As we look at the tape we want to quantify our financial lives. Every inch of the tape measure represents one year of our lives. For example, the marking on  the tape at 20 inches represents our lives at 20 years old, 40 inches would represent 40 years old, and 65 inches would represent 65 years old, and so on. If we live to be 86 years old, the tape would stretch out 86 inches. You get the picture.

7

The first phase in your financial life is the ***accumulation phase***. The accumulation phase starts around age 18 to 20 and continues until the age you retire. This phase of your financial life could be as long as 45 to 50 years. It is in this phase that you begin working and earning your own income. Like its name would suggest, you start accumulating things. With money now in your pocket you can make a few significant purchases. During this phase of your financial life you might buy your first car or first house. Most people start a family during this time of their life.

Remember the tape measure analogy? This accumulation period would obviously be the longest end of the tape because it represents the longest period of time.

Now let's look at how you could invest your money in the accumulation phase, and what type of investments would be suitable. In the accumulation phase of your financial life, time is on your side. Because this phase in your financial life stretches over such a long time frame, just about *any* investment out there could be deemed suitable to be used in this phase. For example, stocks, bonds, mutual funds, CDs, emerging markets, global markets..... All of the above products could be suitable choices in this phase. During this period, you can take on more risk because you have time to make up for any mistakes and losses. Most of us are also working and contributing to retirement savings on a regular basis in this phase of our financial life. The goal is maximum capital appreciation and growth. **"Wall Street"** does a pretty good job of this. (I will use the term "Wall Street" to include most brokers, insurance and financial services registered representatives, brokerage firms, mutual fund companies, and bank's wealth management brokerage departments.) Remember, there is time to overcome the mistakes.

The second phase of your financial life is the ***preservation phase***. You automatically move into this phase when you retire. I realize people retire at different ages, but let's look at the averages. You may retire around 60 and your neighbor at 65. According to the U.S. Census Bureau, the average retirement age in America is 62 years of age[3]. This number has continued to decrease for nearly 100 years, while the average lifespan has gradually increased. In fact, one study concluded that from 1960 to the year 2000, the average life expectancy increased by 7 years, 3.5 of which is attributable to improvements in health care[4]. Retirement as we understand it today is a creation of the modern world. If you retire at the age of 60 and live to be 86 years old, this means you could be spending approximately 26 years in retirement. That's 26 years of living off your retirement savings! Hhhmmm...That's a long time.

It has been my experience working with retirees and those about to retire that something takes place psychologically at some point in the financial preservation time period. It might not happen right away, but I can almost guarantee it will occur. There is usually an uneasiness that the retiree just can't quite identify. This uneasiness usually is the realization that the retiree may run out of money before they run out of life. Until one actually enters the preservation phase, he or she can't fully grasp the pressure of the finality of the situation. I see people every day in my practice that are retired and yet they are still investing their money as if they were in the accumulation phase. These people have almost all their money exposed to the risk of the stock or bond markets. To make things worse they have no protection in place such as stop losses that would mitigate their losses if things turned against them. This is a big mistake!

Let's consider a few of the changes that take place when you retire. First, you are no longer receiving your full salary

---

3 www.census.gov

4 Centers for Medicare and Medicaid Services, Office of the Actuary, National Health Statistics Group, (see Historical, NHE summary including share of GDP, CY 1960-2005, file nhegdp05.zip; and Historical, Projected, NHE Hi storical and projections, 1965-2015, file nhe65-15.zip); cited in http://www.kff.org/insurance/snapshot/chcm030807oth.cfm

or paycheck. Unless you invest wisely and have created your own income stream, you are taking quite a pay cut.

There's also the social security shuffle to worry about. No... it's not the latest dance craze at the local VFW. The social security shuffle occurs when one spouse passes away, leaving the surviving spouse with a lesser income. The government will not continue to issue the household both social security checks. Therefore, the surviving spouse will only receive one income. Uncle Sam kindly gives the surviving spouse the higher of the two checks. However, this spouse is now attempting to pay bills and living expenses on two thirds of the regular household income! If you didn't plan wisely, I believe your beloved will be moving to a new neighborhood. Within today's economy, I can't imagine how anyone can afford to continue their current lifestyle with 1/3 *less* income. If you're used to receiving $3000 per month, but suddenly have to pay the same expenses with only $2000 .... well, you see what I mean. So, you see, you are now relying upon your retirement nest egg to provide you with an income for the rest of your life.

Some of you may say "AHA! I got you on this one, Richard! I will no longer have a mortgage to pay." This is quite true..... but remember in the introduction and first chapter I happened to mention the possibility of paying more for medical and prescription care. What about nursing home care? In my local community, the average monthly fee for basic care at a nursing home is approximately $6,000 each month! What will that amount increase to in 5 years..... 10 years? From 1970 to 1990, nursing home expenditures in the United States increased faster than any other health care cost in this country, with a 12.7 percent annual rate of growth. By 1990, 10.2% of Americans age 75 and older lived in nursing homes.[5] Although that number actually decreased to

---

5 Containing US health care costs: what bullet to bite? – Cost Containment Issues, Methods and Experiences. Health Care Financing Review, Annual 1991 by Stephen F. Jencks, George J. Schreiber.

7.4% by 2006 (due to greater long-term care options for seniors, such as assisted living and home health care) there are still currently more than 1.8 million people living in skilled nursing facilities today[6].

Do you realize the average cost of a nursing home stay is $75,000 per year! And these costs have been rising at a rate of approximately 6% each year. That is a retirement expense that was never contemplated by most seniors, and their financial portfolios could never take that kind of a hit. Government programs like Medicare and Medicaid were not initially designed to handle the number of seniors who are in need of care today.

With the government proposing revising the national budget by cutting Medicare/Medicaid programs, we all have to entertain the idea that we will be paying more for daily care in our senior years than our monthly mortgage ever was! Just because the average American in living longer doesn't necessarily mean we will do so in good health or without the need for assistance. I'm not trying to keep you awake tonight with such thoughts……. I myself consider these factors in my own planning….. I'm simply trying to help you understand that just because we finally make it to the top of Mt Everest doesn't mean the struggle is over. We still have to descend the mountain!

Now, let's go back to the tape measure picture. What is the difference between the accumulation phase length of the tape and the preservation phase length of the tape? That is correct. The preservation phase of the tape is *much shorter* than the accumulation phase of the tape! Time is no longer on your side. You cannot afford to make mistakes and lose your money. You do not have a lengthy recovery period to regain financial loss. That's why it is paramount to your success that you understand this concept. You have to invest your money differently! I have found that "Wall Street" does

---

[6] Fewer seniors live in nursing homes, USA TODAY, 9/27/2007, Haya El Nasser.

The Fleecing of America's Baby Boomers

not understand the preservation phase. They just seem to concentrate on growth. I'll talk more about this in detail in another chapter.

Finally, we all enter the third phase of our financial life called the **distribution phase** when our life is over and we meet our maker. You and I will leave this world with the same amount of money that billionaire Sam Walton took with him; none. Although the actual distribution phase occurs after you are gone, it is very important that we direct careful attention to this financial phase while we are alive.

Haven't considered the distribution of your assets yet? It's OK. No worries. You already have a distribution plan. Even if you *haven't* made a plan, you already have a plan. It's the John Q. Public distribution plan! And you can bet your bottom dollar that your loved ones, your church, or your charities are not at the head of the list to receive what you leave behind. Without a clearly stated estate plan, the government gets to decide how your remaining wealth is distributed. Do you really want a bunch of politicians and outdated laws to make such decisions for you! The current economy is raw proof of what the government does with financial assets. I know I don't want the government mishandling what I have worked my entire existence to accumulate!

To avoid such a catastrophe, you will need to put forth a little more effort on your part. I know, I KNOW... Our own nonexistence is not something we want to think about. But anything worthwhile takes effort. And, as your grandfather might have said, "If you want something done right, you have to do it yourself!" –This means **you** will need to do some estate planning to ensure that your wishes are carried out instead of letting the state do it for you. A recent survey found that 43 percent of workers spent more time planning for their most recent vacation than planning for retirement.[7]

---

[7] "When It Comes to Saving for Retirement, Average Americans Are Resigned to Muddling Through ... Alone," October 3, 2008, www.aarpfinancial.com.

People are spending more time planning and researching for their one week vacation than they do planning for a 26 year retirement and their estate plan which could create stable financial security for their families!

Estate Planning is defined as: *the arranging for the disposition and management of one's estate at death through the use of wills, trusts, insurance policies, and other devices*[8] Basic estate planning is simply making sure that what you own goes to who you want, in the most tax efficient manner possible. Sounds simple enough... right? The catch here is that the rules of estate planning have changed AND they will keep changing as long as politicians stay in Washington! The language in past wills no longer has the same effect it may have had 5+ years ago. Actually, a simple will is not enough. Oh! And here's a good one.... The Power of Attorney you had created for a medical crisis can legally prohibit your will from being executed properly! That's right. You heard me. Because of law changes and shifts in the government, your very own Power of Attorney, which YOU created, can be the one legal document that renders your accounts penniless even before you die!

Hhhmmmm..... Has your advisor made you aware of these nightmarish factors? Has your advisor been proactive in helping you accomplish your goals? Do they understand the different phases of your financial life? Will you succeed? You have to know the rules to win.

Is it that your advisor doesn't know or they just don't care? It's starting to get interesting!

---

8 Merriam-Webster's Dictionary of Law, © 1996 Merriam-Webster, Inc.

CHAPTER 3:
HOW DID WE GET INTO THIS MESS?

"These are the times that try men's souls."
- Thomas Paine "The Crisis" (1776-77)

The United States of America is in financial crisis! You would be hard-pressed to find anyone who would disagree with that statement. Just this weekend, the gasoline prices in my neighborhood jumped 14 cents per gallon overnight! Houses for sale in the most desirable neighborhoods are sitting vacant for months due to the poor market conditions. What's going on? How did the economy spiral out of control so much as to create our current state of crisis?

In January of 2010, I attended a meeting in San Diego. This gathering of an elite group of advisors in my industry provided me with an honest, and ugly, understanding of America's economic status. One of the keynote speakers at this event  was David Walker. If the name isn't familiar to you, David Walker served as the Comptroller General of the United States of America and the head of the Government Accountability Office (GOA) from 1998 to 2008. Mr. Walker was appointed by President Clinton and served under both Democratic and Republican administrations. He was essentially the federal government's chief auditor and head accountant.

Mr. Walker is the Founder and CEO of the Comeback America Initiative. I would recommend that everyone watch the eighty-two minute documentary film entitled, **I.O.U.S.A.** (You can find it online; just Google it.)

Mr. Walker has conducted a wake-up tour across the United States to bring attention to the governments unsustainable spending. In his speech, Mr. Walker stressed that the United States needs to get its fiscal house in order. And it is critical to do so immediately! "The United States government does not have a revenue problem, it has a spending problem!" At the time of this writing, our national debt is over $14 trillion and it is increasing at the alarming rate of over $100 million an hour!

To give you some idea of how large a number that is, let's translate it into something that we're all familiar with, time. How long is a period of time represented by one million seconds? The answer is about 11 1/2 days. How long would you say one billion seconds represent? The answer is about 32 years. Do you know how long one trillion seconds represent? The answer is around 32,000 years![9] I didn't stutter.....you heard me correctly: thirty-two thousand years! That is an incredibly large number. If you were to pay down our debt $1 per second, it would take 32,000 YEARS to pay off $1 trillion. Therefore, to pay the current national debt in full, it would take approximately 448,000 **YEARS**!! (14 x 32,000). .....Now, that's without the debt growing any further; nor does it include interest!

Still can't fully comprehend the absurdity of our national debt?!?! Check out the following comparisons:[10]

---

9 http://www.defeatthedebt.com/understanding-the-national-debt/millions-billions-trillions/

10 http://www.defeatthedebt.com/understanding-the-national-debt/millions-billions-trillions/

How Did We Get Into This Mess?

- A trillion $10 bills, taped end to end, would wrap around the Earth more than 380 times. The length of a $10 bill (6.14 in) divided into the equatorial circumference of Earth in inches (24,901 miles x 5,280 ft per mile x 12 inches per foot = 1,577,727,360) yields the number of $10 bills it takes to circle the Earth once (256,958,853.42 $10 bills). {[1577727360 / 6.140 (length of dollar bill)] = 256,958,853.42.}.
This number of $10 bills is equal to $2,569,588,534.20 (around $2.57 billion). [10 x 256958853.4 = 2569588534] To find the number of round-the-Earth trips needed to raise that amount of money to $1 trillion, divide the trillion by this number and the result is 389.167. [1,000,000,000,000/ (2569588534.2) = 389.167]
- That's a ton of cash—actually 1.1 million tons of it.
There are approximately 907,185 grams in a ton [2000 x 453.59237 (grams in a pound) = 907,184.74 grams in a ton]. If one dollar bill weighs one gram, then 907,185 dollar bills equal one ton. Therefore, one trillion dollar bills equal 1,102,311 tons of cash. [1,000,000,000,000 / 907,185 = 1102310.99]
- It would take more than 10,000 18-wheelers to transport one trillion $1 bills. Our national debt today would fill up 30 of the largest container ships ever constructed, each holding more than 4,100 containers full of cash. Using the Department of Transportation's standards for a 53-foot shipping container (8.0 feet wide, 8.5 feet high, 53 feet long), the volume of a shipping container is roughly 3604 cubic feet.
Using the dimensions of a dollar bill (6.14 in. x 2.61 in. x .0043 in.), the volume of one dollar bill is .0000396 cubic feet. Therefore, one 53-foot container would hold roughly 91 million bills. [3604 cu. ft. / .000039 = 91,010,110]
One trillion $1 bills would therefore fill more than 10,000 tractor trailers. [1,000,000,000,000 / 91,010,101 = 10,987.79]

The world's largest cargo ship, the Emma Maersk, can carry 11,000 "20-foot Equivalent Unit" shipping containers (TEUs), and a 53-foot container is considered 2.65 TEUs.

Therefore roughly 4,151 53-foot containers [11,000 / 2.65 = 4150.94 53 ft containers] will fit on this cargo ship.

10,987 shipping containers would fill two and one-half of the largest container ships ever made, or three average container ships. [10,987 / 4,151 = 2.64] Our national debt of $12 trillion would fill more than 30 such container ships. [12 x 2.65 = 31.8]

- You could spend $10 million a day and it would still take you 273 years to spend $1 trillion.

At a rate of 10 million dollars a day, it would take a person 100,000 days to spend one trillion dollars. 100,000 days is 273 years. {[$1,000,000,000,000 / $10,000,000 = 100,000 days] / 365.2425 days = 273 years}

The national debt, at the time of this writing, breaks down to over $128,000 per taxpayer.[11] Do you have an extra $128,000 you want to throw at it? Neither do I. If you want to really get the true picture, we need to look at the total unfunded liabilities of the United States. The future unfunded liability which includes Social Security, Medicare, Medicaid, and the Prescription Drug program is over $113 trillion at this writing. That represents a liability of over $1 million per taxpayer.

If you would like to track these numbers, you can try to keep up with the numbers at www.usdebtclock.org. I say 'try' because when you actually go to this site, the rate at which the numbers change will leave you in an unsettled moment of "Awe".

---

11 www.usdebtclock.org

I think we all could heed the advice of an old cowboy:

"When you find yourself in a hole, quit digging!"
-Will Rogers

In the next chapter we will explore some of the things that *are* in our control. Put your thinking cap on and let's get on with it.

CHAPTER 4:
WHAT CAN YOU CONTROL?

It doesn't do us any good to spend our time and energy concerned about things that are out of our control. Should we never enjoy a warm summer's rain for fear of a hurricane? Do we completely avoid beach vacations just in case a sudden tsunami hits the coastline? Have we ever told our children not to go out for the team because they may not make the cut? No!

Now, I am definitely not saying to live without a care in the world..... to throw caution to the wind! Absolutely not! My lesson here is that we prepare the best we can by gathering knowledge, training our bodies and minds, or enlisting the help of accomplished specialists to guide us in our decision making. This pertains to every aspect of our lives, and especially in our financial life!

That being said, there are several common sense strategies that you can use to enhance your financial future. You just need to understand these strategies and implement them.

Taxes

The first strategy we will look at is reducing or eliminating **unnecessary taxes**. Now right off the bat I know you're thinking the only two things that are certain in life are death and taxes. I would have to agree with you on those two points. However, there are people paying *unnecessary* taxes every day. These taxes are avoidable. You noticed I said avoid; not evade. You know the difference between tax avoidance and tax evasion? The answer is 20 years in prison. (That was a little joke. Even financial advisors can be funny! ….No?)

Let's begin with the 1099 tax form. The Internal Revenue Service, which is responsible for collecting and processing tax payments in the United States, uses the 1099 form series to record income other than salaried wages.[12] Though the 1099 MISC Form is the most popular, there are several versions of the 1099. The 1099 INT is utilized to denote the interest on investments that may have been paid in a particular tax year. Form 1099-DIV must be used by taxpayers to report any dividends received from investments, such as stocks. In the United States, when money from a retirement fund is distributed to a person, this is considered a form of income and must be reported to the Internal Revenue Service. Form 1099-R was created for the proper reporting of this money and for determining whether the proper amount of tax has been collected.

The 1099 miscellaneous interest is reported on line 8a of your federal tax return, form 1040. Your dividends received from investments such as stocks are usually reported on line 9a of the federal 1040 form. This is added into your total taxable income for the tax year.

If you are not spending this interest and dividend income, why are you paying tax on it? Did you know if you're receiving Social Security you could also be increasing the tax you pay on your Social Security Benefits. By changing *where* your money is invested, you may be able to reduce your overall tax liability significantly by eliminating 1099 income. You could be deferring the taxes until you actually spend the money. In realizing this important fact, you may be able to reduce taxes on the interest you earn every year. If you're receiving Social Security benefits and you're in a situation where you

---

12 http://search.irs.gov/web/query.html?col=allirs&charset=utf-8&qp=&qs=-Wct%3A%22Internal+Revenue+Manual%22&qc=&qm=0&rf=0&oq=&qt=1099

have to pay taxes on part of those benefits because you have too much retirement income, a significant tax savings may be achieved by reducing taxes on your Social Security income as well.

Has your current advisor helped you reduce unnecessary taxes? If they have not helped you reduce unnecessary taxes, why?

Is it that your advisor doesn't know, or they just don't care?

Fees

The second strategy that we will explore is reducing or eliminating *fees*. According to the featured article in the Money section of the USA Today newspaper dated January 7, 2010, there was 367 billion dollars paid **in fees** to mutual fund money managers from 1999 through 2009. What kind of return do you think the investors received for their $367 billion fee?? Would you believe those investors received the average return of only 1.1% per year. I'll say it again. Only 1.1% per year. Were you one of those people?? Did you know you could have beaten those returns if you had placed that same money into CD's without paying the fees. It is sad to say that most people don't comprehend what they're paying in fees per year. Do you know how much you're paying? Have you ever stopped to think about reducing your fees? Are you paying for bad advice? Let's pull back the curtain and take a good hard look at fees hidden in investments that you may not be aware even exist.

In a Wall Street Journal article dated March 3, 2010, Morningstar Inc. reported on the hidden cost of mutual funds.[13] The article states that the average US stock mutual

---

13 Wall Street Journal online: http://online.wsj.com/article_email/
SB10001424052748703382904575059690954870722-lMyQjAxM-

fund has an operating expense ratio of 1.3% of the assets in the fund. But the article goes on to reveal that is not the real bottom line. The article states that portfolio managers can rack up steep additional expenses buying and selling securities in the fund, but that burden isn't reflected in the standard expense ratio of the fund. These trading costs go unreported because of the complexity in tracking such expenses due to the hidden nature of such fees. A study of thousands of US stock mutual funds completed put the average cost of the buying and selling of securities at 1.44% of the total assets of the fund, with an average of 0.14% at the bottom of the ranks and 2.96% at the top! "Expenses are one of the most important things investors can look at," says study co-author Richard Evans, an assistant professor of finance at the University of Virginia's Darden School.[14]

How can this be, you ask? Well, a lot of times the fees and expenses of the mutual fund are similar to that of an iceberg. Odd comparison?? Not really when you stop to consider what part of an iceberg is visible? If you think back to the sinking of the historic Titanic, you'll realize the largest part of an iceberg is below the surface where you cannot see it. The same is true with many mutual funds. You can actually see the published cost of the expense ratios in their sales material, but the true cost in the fund is much greater than it appears. I have included the following illustration to give you a visual perspective of what I'm talking about when it comes to the hidden fees and costs.

There is an old saying; "A picture is worth thousand words". In this case, a picture could save you thousands of dollars!

TAwMDAwMTEwNDEyWj.html?source=patrick.net#

[14] Wall Street Journal online: http://online.wsj.com/article_email/SB10001424052748703382904575059690954870722-lMyQjAxM-TAwMDAwMTEwNDEyWj.html?source=patrick.net#

What Can YOU Control?

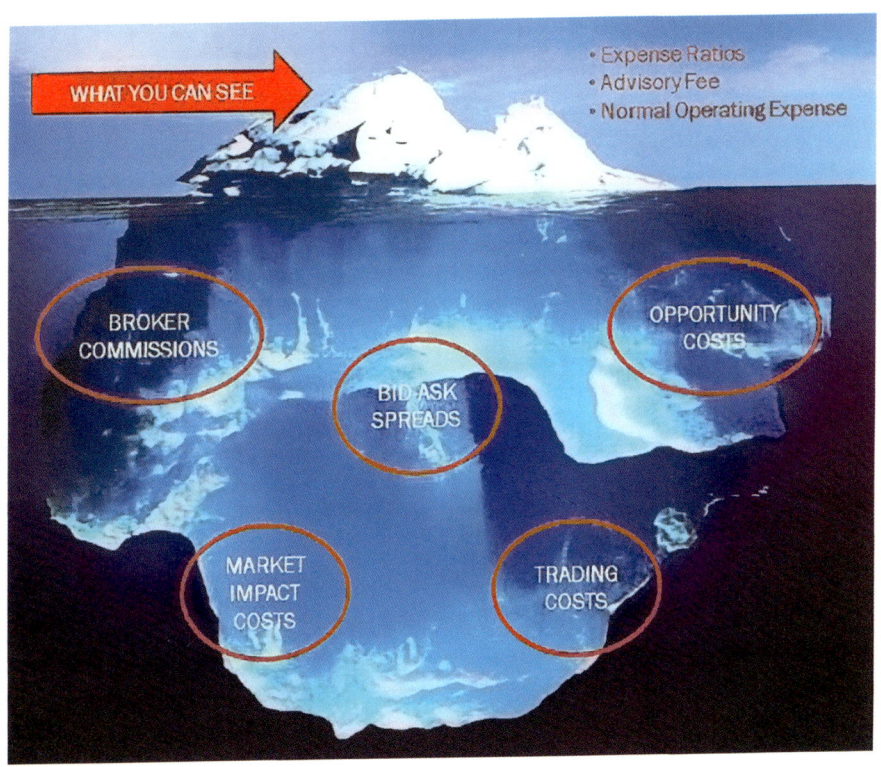

"That's not the real bottom line. There are other costs not reported in the expense ratio related to the buying and selling of securities in the portfolio – and those expenses can make a fund **two to three times as costly** as advertised."
 – **Wall Street Journal and Morningstar, Inc. March 3, 2010**

Dr. Burton Malkiel, who has a Harvard MBA, a PhD. from Princeton University, professor of finance at Princeton University, and the author of the books *"A Random Walk Down Wall Street"* and *"The Elements of Investing"*, believes paying close attention to the fees you're paying is critical to your investing success. Dr. Malkiel states that most people have no idea the amount of fees they're paying. Investors need to understand the same investment objective can be accomplished at a much lower cost by using index funds and exchange traded funds. Dr. Burton Malkiel believes you may be able to accomplish investment in the stock market for as little as 1/10 of 1% annual cost in fees.

Wow! What a benefit to the investor! Why wouldn't you want to save 1 to 3% yearly on the cost of your investments, just by reducing your fees? This savings is such a grand positive impact to the bottom line every year and really adds up over time.

What is your advisor doing to reduce your fees? Is your advisor utilizing low-cost index funds and exchange traded funds in your portfolio whenever possible? If not; why not?

Is it that your advisor doesn't know, or they just don't care?

The Stock Market

Have you ever invested in the stock market? If your answer to that question is yes, there's a good chance that you have lost money at one time or another. There is also a good chance that you *made* some money at one time or another. Let's take a quick review of some simple basic terms when investing in the stock market. When the market trend is up, it's called a *bull*. When the market trend is down, it's called a *bear*. Now the golden rule for success in the stock market is that you *buy low* and *sell high*. Isn't it strange? Just about everybody knows the basic rules and the terminology used for investing in the stock market. And yet, very few are successful. So what's the problem? As Dr. Phil would say, "How's that working out for you"?

Remember how we were talking about things we can control? Note to self:: *We cannot control the stock market*. The stock market is going to do what the stock market does. We have absolutely no control over whether the stock's values go up or down. I certainly cannot tell you what the stock market is going to do on any given day. My crystal ball broke a few years back.

What Can YOU Control?

For example, one of the largest single- day drops in the value of the stock market was caused not by anything to do with United States stocks, but with the devaluation of Chinese stocks. Referred to as **Black Monday,** October 19, 1987, is when stock markets around the world crashed, shedding a huge value in a very short time. The crash began in Hong Kong and spread west through international time zones to Europe, hitting the United States after other markets had already declined by a significant margin. The Dow Jones Industrial Average (DJIA) dropped by 508 points to 1738.74 (22.61%).[15] A degree of mystery is associated with the 1987 crash. Important assumptions concerning human rationality, the efficient-market hypothesis, and economic equilibrium were brought into question by the event. Debate as to the cause of the crash still continues many years after the event, with no firm conclusions reached.

Although we have no power to command the market, the one thing we can control is how much of our hard-earned money is invested in the stock market. Simply put: When your money is invested in the stock market, your money is at risk of being lost. A lot of people only concentrate on the upside potential when investing in the stock market.

Most people believe they *have* to invest in the stock market to make money. That idea is drilled into their heads by the investment pundits they see on TV. They do not understand that the market cycles every few years. A lot of people just invest and hope it works. This is a mistake! Don't get me wrong, I like the stock market. However, you must respect it. ..... Similar to the ocean.... We want to have fun and play in the surf, but we must respect the power of the wave and the threat of the undertow.

---

15 Browning, E.S. (2007-10-15). "Exorcising Ghosts of Octobers Past". *The Wall Street Journal* (Dow Jones & Company): pp. C1–C2. http://online.wsj.com/article/SB119239926667758592.html?mod=mkts_main_news_hs_h. Retrieved 2007-10-15.

We are in a new paradigm with modern investing. The old advice of just buy some good stocks or mutual funds and hold them doesn't work. Does your advisor understand how the changed dynamic affects your success?

Is it that your advisor doesn't know or they just don't care?

True Diversification vs. Asset Allocation

Diversification means reducing risk by investing in a variety of assets –Wikipedia.

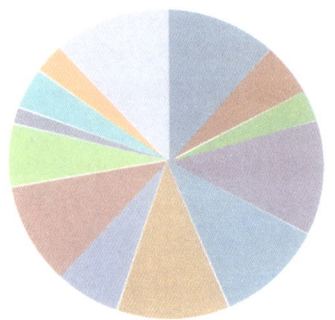

I want to examine the concept of true diversification versus asset allocation. When talking to most brokers or bank employee investment management people about investing your money, this question always seems to arise, "What kind of an investor are you?" If you cannot give them a categorical answer such as I'm moderate, aggressive, or conservative, you end up with the second question. "Well, how do you feel about risk?" After several questions and possibly filling out a risk questionnaire, they all wind up at the same destination. They get out their pie chart.

While referring to their handy-dandy chart, they propose that you "win the game" by owning a little bit of everything. You need some small-cap stocks, mid-cap stocks, large-cap stocks, value stocks, growth stocks, emerging markets stocks, and some international stocks. Or stock mutual funds, which might contain a combination of any of the above, coupled with some *fixed income* investments. These fixed income investments may come in the form of corporate bonds, treasury bonds, high yield bonds, collateralized mortgage obligations, or bond mutual funds, which could be made up of all the above. They may even throw in a little cash or some CDs. (Whew!) This is pretty much the general consensus advice

What Can YOU Control?

you would get from "Wall Street". If you follow their suggestions, they will then pronounce your portfolio *"**diversified**"*. .....Remember that word - diversified.

Have you been in one of these meetings already? Let me guess, ... you've seen the handy-dandy pie chart too, right? This seems to be quite a problem in the investment business. This 'cookie cutter attitude' that if we put a bit of everything in your portfolio we've done our best to cover all our bases..... Wait a minute..... the financial advisor should not be worried about covering 'their bases' ..... they *should* be focused on what the best plan is for you and your personal situation!

This is one of the areas I think "Wall Street" is wrong! I believe they confuse the term *diversification* with *asset allocation*. Asset allocation involves dividing an investment portfolio among different asset categories, such as stocks, bonds, and cash. The process of determining which mix of assets to hold in your portfolio is a very personal one. The asset allocation that works best for you at any given point in your life will depend largely on your time horizon and your ability to tolerate risk.

Can you lose money in a diversified account? Yes! I believe to have true diversification in your investment portfolio, your investments should actually be divided into two categories, **safe** and **risk**.

First, let's define what a safe investment is. I believe the website www.SafeMoneyPlaces.com is one of the best consumer educational websites available for educating yourself on the meaning of a safe investment.

"A safe money investment is one where your principal is protected from loss as long as you follow the initial guidelines, and if you decide to take your money and leave, you pretty much know what it's going to cost you."-**SafeMoneyPlaces.com**

Based on that definition, there are only four places that are actually safe: CD's, insured deposits, savings bonds, and fixed annuities. Please Note: That's fixed annuities *not* variable annuities.

The Fleecing of America's Baby Boomers

Wow, that's a far cry from what "Wall Street" calls safe! Wall Street touts safe investments as fixed income. Can you lose money in fixed income? Can you say Lehman Brothers, Countrywide Financial Corp., mortgage backed securities, or collateralized mortgage obligations? You can lose your shirt investing in so called highly rated, investment grade fixed income. Just because it's a fixed income product doesn't mean it's safe. Heck, even the United States government stepped right in front of the bondholders when they took over General Motors Corporation! These bond holders found out the hard way why a fixed income product with an investment rated security does not mean a guaranteed income!

The pie charts below are a good example of what a true diversified portfolio should look like with the assets divided into designated 'safe' and 'risk' categories.

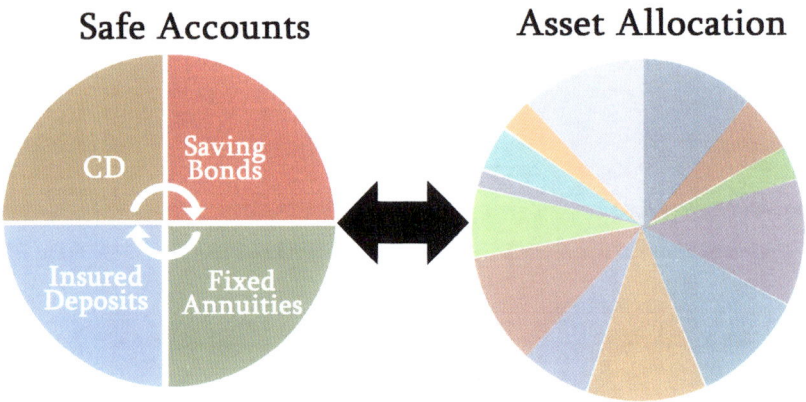

Asset allocation is an extremely important discipline to be utilized for the risk side of the portfolio. It can enhance performance and reduce some of the risk; however it cannot eliminate all the risk. It's kind of like being "a little bit pregnant", either you are or you are not.

What Can YOU Control?

The bottom line is: Your money is either *at risk* or it is *not at risk*. The money that is invested in the safe account portion has no risk. It cannot lose value. Think about it. You will never open your statement and see a loss! You won't have to wonder why your broker doesn't call when your account drops 40%. This approach to investing provides a peace of mind that comes with a successful, secure retirement.

Albert Einstein defined insanity as doing the same things over and over and expecting different results.

"Just hang in there; it always comes back." **Oh, really?** Well we won't bring up or talk about Enron or WorldCom which were once darlings of the stock market.

"Just hang in there; it always comes back." **Does it?**

Is it that your advisor doesn't know or they just don't care?

31

CHAPTER 5:
THE AGE 100 RULES

Now that you understand that your overall portfolio should be divided into safe and risk components, the question which now arises is: What percentage of your investment dollars should be in the safe component sector and how much of those dollars should be allocated into the risk component sector?

A rule of thumb that has been around for a long time is the "Age 100 Rule". The age 100 rule states that you should subtract your age from 100 to calculate which percentage of your portfolio should be at risk. For example, if you're 70 years of age, only 30% of your assets should be at risk. That means that 70% of your assets should be in safe investments. The age 100 rule is a great standard to follow when you're in the *preservation* phase of your financial life. This simple rule protects mature portfolios from losing too much money. This simple guideline can be the difference between having a safe, secure retirement and not being able to retire at all!

As I mentioned earlier, "Wall Street" doesn't quite understand this concept. "Wall Street" has a different definition of safety. Let me give you an example of what I'm talking about. In March of 2000, the tech bubble burst. Which investments did "Wall Street" run to for safety? They hid out in the so-called safe investments of financials and real estate. In 2008, which investments got taken out, shot in the head and thrown under the bus? That's right, those so-called safe investments of financials and real estate!

Remember, *"A safe money investment is one where your principal is protected from loss as long as you follow the initial guidelines, and if you decide to take your money and leave, you pretty much know what it's going to cost you."* No ifs, ands, or buts. If it doesn't fit this definition... **it is not safe**!

A slight variation in the Age 100 rule is the Age 120 rule. Because people are now living longer, some believe that you should have more of your investments on the risk side. Therefore, you should subtract your age from 120 to get the percentage of your portfolio that should be at risk. Keep in mind, these numbers and percentages are not cut in stone, but they are good rules of thumb to follow. Outside factors, such as health or lifestyle, will cause each of us to look at those guidelines in our own unique way.

Let's now look how this rule fits into your overall investment plan. What is the most important component to the building of a strong house? It's the foundation. If the foundation is not solid, the house will not be stable. If the foundation is weak, small cracks (that are unnoticeable at first) will eventually give way to major damage.

Everything else can be perfect, but have a flaw in the foundation, and you're house could collapse and be worthless. The same is true when building your investment portfolio. Take a look at the pyramid of investing chart.

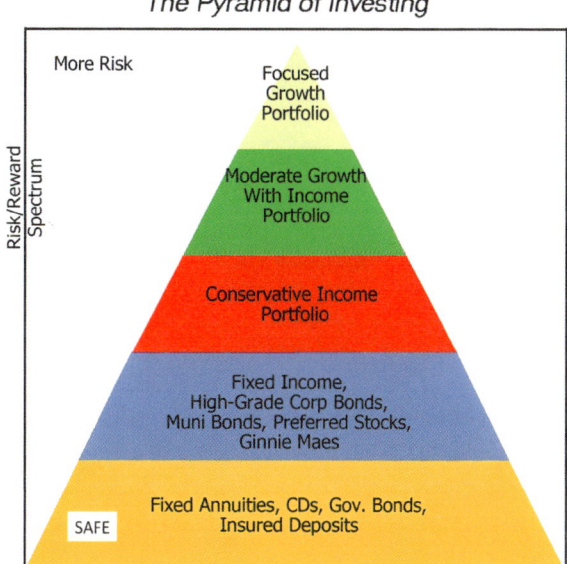

The Pyramid of Investing

- Focused Growth Portfolio
- Moderate Growth With Income Portfolio
- Conservative Income Portfolio
- Fixed Income, High-Grade Corp Bonds, Muni Bonds, Preferred Stocks, Ginnie Maes
- Fixed Annuities, CDs, Gov. Bonds, Insured Deposits (SAFE)

More Risk — Risk/Reward Spectrum

Notice at the base of the pyramid, you will find the *safe investments*. This is the bed rock that any sound investment portfolio is built upon. As you travel up the pyramid towards the top, investments become more risky. As with most things in life, it is imperative that you start with a strong base or foundation.

CHAPTER 6: DOLLARS-VS-PERCENTAGES

Have you ever wondered why it's so difficult to get ahead when investing in the stock market? Does it seem like Wall Street takes it away fast and gives it back slow? Have you ever been told by your advisor or broker, "You're up X% this month!" But when you look at how much money you had when you opened the account –vs- where you are now, there's less money? How can this be? What are you missing??

That's because a lot of people do not understand the differences between dollars and percentages when it comes to investing!

**IT's OKAY. You're not alone.
Let me help you out a little……**

Let's look at an example: We will use $100,000 because it's easy to do the math. You invest $100,000 in the stock market and the market goes down 40% in one year. (*That has happened more than once in a ten year span,* 2000 – 2010). How much do you have left? That's right, $60,000. Now let's turn around and say the market goes right back up 40% the next year. How much do you have now? Well 40% of $60,000 is $24,000 added to your $60,000 equals $84,000. You still haven't quite recovered, but technically you are up in your percentages.

37

If the market lost 40% in one year, and you followed the "just hang in there" rule, then the market went back up 40% the next year.... you still would not have all your money back! You see, percentages and dollars are different! After a 40% loss, the market would have to come back **67%** for you to be back to $100,000. The math gets a little tricky, especially with our current economy.

Keep in mind, the market runs in cycles. This type of investing actually becomes a matter of timing. Will you have in enough time in your financial life phase to be able to make up for previous losses before the market cycles down again?

"Today's investor does not profit from yesterday's growth."

Warren Buffett

I've seen some advisors trying to put lipstick on a pig. That's what I call it when they run a report showing you having a nice increase in a certain time period, but you still lost money over the life of the account. It is important that you know the *real rate of return* in your account. Track how your account is doing overall not just in a certain shorter period of time.

The stock market wiped out five years of growth in approximately 10 trading days in 2008.

If you're retired, when the market goes down, do you quit taking your income? Do you reduce the amount of your withdrawal? How does this affect your nest egg? Does this increase the chance of you running out of money? These are valid concerns that should be addressed.

You might start asking yourself, "Am I going to run out of money? Can I make up the losses?" Again, these are all legitimate questions that come to mind when the market turns down.

You might think of Will Rogers' famous quote:

"I'm interested more in the return of my money, than the return on my money." – Will Rogers

Have you repeatedly lost money in the stock market when there is a downturn? Do you feel that something should have been done to prevent the loss from being so large? What did your advisor do to protect you from loss in the stock market? Isn't this their livelihood? Shouldn't they have the knowledge and skills to protect what you've worked your whole life to accumulate??

Here's a tip that you probably already know but don't think about too much: Most investors are controlled by two emotions, fear and greed. We just accept the fact that the individual we are handing our money over to is fueled by one of these two factors. I mean, what are you going to do?........ This is just how life is...... Right?... It's just one of those outside factors we can't control and shouldn't worry about. Really??

Is it that your advisor doesn't know or they just don't care?

There are other behaviors that influence our decisions.

CHAPTER 7: BEHAVIORAL ECONOMICS

Almost every aspect of the human life has been analyzed in one way or the other. There have been studies that range from why people are attracted to other people; to what colors influence our moods. Millions of research dollars are spent each year to see what type of coffee cup Starbucks customers would prefer or how the shelves at Walmart should be at eye level for particular products. So it's no surprise that there have also been several studies conducted that look into why people behave the way they do when it comes to investing. These studies have identified behaviors that exist in investors and affect the way they make decisions that are not necessarily in their best interest. Quite frankly, these behaviors can keep investors from being successful. Let's take a look at a few behaviors and how they could affect an investment decision.

Confirmation Bias

"We look for information that confirms our decisions, not conflict with them."

In one study people were shown a restaurant and asked to rate this restaurant on a scale of 1 to 10 based upon how they thought the restaurant *would* meet their expectations. The "customers" were then sent into the restaurant to eat. The participants in the study purposely were served poor food and received bad service. *After* their dining experience these panel members were then asked to rate the restaurant again. The participants were very reluctant to change their original rating of eight or nine to a lower rating even after they experienced poor food and bad service. Their minds were automatically searching for information that would confirm their original decision was correct. They did not want to conflict with their original ratings. Interesting isn't it?

Have you ever bought a new car that you thought was a unique color? You didn't think that there were many cars on the road that were that same color. Yet all of a sudden, when you drove down the road, you recognize there were several cars that color. You just confirmed your decision. Even knowing this response exists, I fell victim of this myself when I purchased my first car... a white Chevy Monte Carlo with a black landau roof. I knew there weren't many of those on the road. I never saw them much……. To my dismay, I saw at least 2 per day after purchasing that vehicle! I duped myself!

Short Term Memory Syndrome

"We remember short-term gains and forget historical losses and cycles."

This is a very common behavior. Why did people who lost a tremendous amount of money in the stock market in 2000, turn around and do the exact same thing in the decline of 2008? You see, investors remember and concentrate on the short-term trend and they forget about things that happened in the past. They believe that the most recent trends will continue indefinitely, and forget about long-term cycles. If the short-term trend is up, it will continue to go up; and if the short-term trend is down, it will continue to go down.

Status Quo Bias

"We have the tendency to avoid making changes."

People do not like change. We are creatures of habit. It seems the older we get, the less we like change. I'm sure you've heard the old saying,"We do it this way because that's the way we've always done it." The same is true for people when it comes to investing their money. It's hard for them to change. What drives the fear of change? There are people who know that their existing financial plan is not going to work but are afraid to change it. I believe a lot of it stems from not having the correct information to make an educated decision.

Decision Paralysis

"We have too many choices, so we do NOTHING!"

People exhibit this behavior every day. We are constantly bombarded with information throughout the day, especially when it comes to money. Let's say you turned on CNBC at 7 AM in the morning and you watched until five o'clock in the afternoon, how many different ideas do you think you would receive on investing your money? If you would actually do this as an experiment, you'd find it's information overload!

When an individual has too many options, that person just throws their hands in the air and say, "Forget it!" They are just exhausted from trying to calculate their best option and weighing all the information. Unfortunately, this 'decision paralysis' also prevents people from making positive changes that need to be made in their retirement accounts.

Sunk Cost Fallacy

"People will hold their investments until they are worth almost NOTHING!"

It's surprising how many investors exhibit this behavior. Let's say an investor owns shares in Company XYZ. Now XYZ stock value has fallen 20%. It is losing market share, has poor management, and its delivery of product to market is inferior to its competitor company ABC. When it is suggested to the investor that they should sell the shares of Company XYZ and purchase company ABC, which is dominating the marketplace, the response of the investor is, "I will sell XYZ and buy ABC as soon as the value of the shares of stock in Company XYZ gets back to where I bought it."

After the value of XYZ falls another 30% the investor's excuse for not making any changes became, "I might as well hold on to it. I've lost this much, I might as well lose it all!"

Anchoring

"We are influenced by media and get stuck on reference points."

After the market decline in 2008, and when the market started recovering, how much time was spent in the media discussing each thousand point milestone as the Dow Jones industrial average started moving back up?

The media becomes fixated upon each level. Each and every time the Dow reaches one of the thousand point levels the media starts obsessing all over again. Will the market break this level today? Will it close above the thousand point milestone? How long will it take to regain the level now that it has fallen below it? On and on and on again, day after day!

If we're honest with ourselves we know that we are influenced by behavioral economics. It is important that we understand how these economic behaviors influence our decisions.

I hope this brief explanation has given you some insight as to how you can become a better investor. By understanding these behaviors and recognizing when we begin exhibitingthese behaviors, we can make better, educated decisions. Lord knows we need all the help we can get!

Have you ever had a discussion about these behavioral tendencies with *your* advisor?

Is it that your advisor doesn't know or they just don't care?

CHAPTER 8:
INCOME PLANNING

Having an income plan that provides you with a *guaranteed* income that you *cannot outlive* is critical to you having a successful and worry free retirement.

I have to tell you.... this is where most advisors miss the boat. As I mentioned in an earlier chapter, "Wall Street" is pretty good in the accumulation phase when time is on your side. But they just haven't woken up to the fact that fixed income does not allow you to have a guaranteed income because it doesn't meet our previous definition of safety.

The "Wall Street" philosophy seems to focus on the growth of your assets, rather than the preservation of your assets and the fact that these assets will be providing you with income. They seem to have forgotten you will not always be in the accumulation phase in your financial life. Once you start living off of your assets in the preservation phase of your financial life, income becomes more important. You cannot afford to lose any of your principle. Do you remember the investment matrix from a previous chapter? That was the matrix that started with your safe investments at the bottom of the foundation and went up to the top of the pyramid with the most risky investments. Let's take a look at the investment matrix alongside your expense matrix.

On your expense matrix your normal everyday living expenses are at the foundation or base. These are the expenses that have to be covered, such as food, clothing and paying your bills. As you move up the pyramid you have expenses that would become more of an option such as travel, gifts, projects, and hobbies.

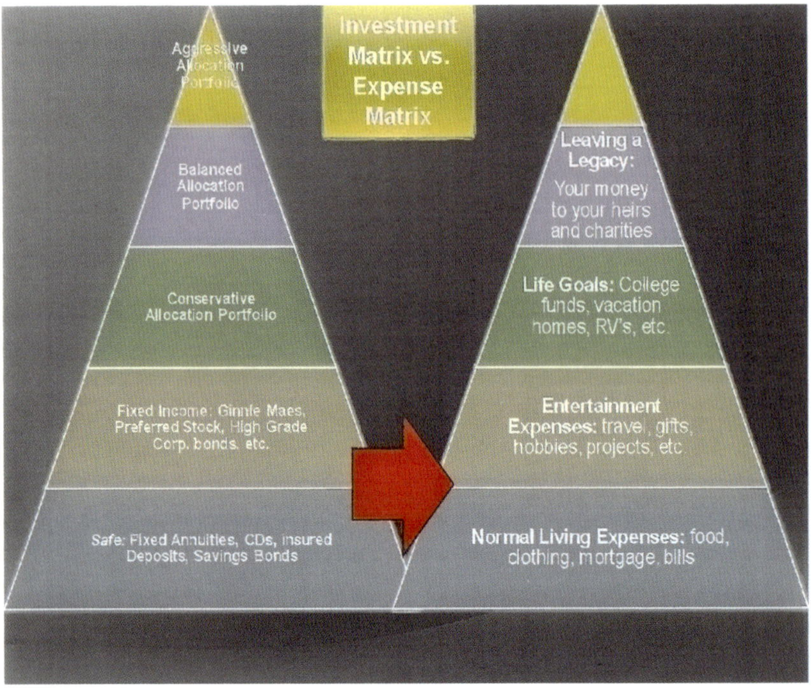
Investment Matrix vs. Expense Matrix
Balanced Allocation Portfolio
Conservative Allocation Portfolio
Fixed Income: Ginnie Maes, Preferred Stock, High Grade Corp. bonds, etc.
Safe: Fixed Annuities, CDs, insured Deposits, Savings Bonds
Leaving a Legacy: Your money to your heirs and charities
Life Goals: College funds, vacation homes, RV's, etc.
Entertainment Expenses: travel, gifts, hobbies, projects, etc.
Normal Living Expenses: food, clothing, mortgage, bills

You want to make sure that your normal living expenses are more than covered by your safe investments to provide you with a guaranteed income that you cannot outlive. This gives you the peace of mind that your lifestyle will not be interrupted due to a turn down in the market or an investment that went south. This allows you to concentrate on the really important things in life; like enjoying your retirement!

Do you have an income plan that provides you with the security of never running out of money no matter how long you live? Is your income plan dependent upon a stock dividend or a bond yield that is not guaranteed? Is your income plan tied to a variable you cannot control? If you are uncertain, you need to get your house in order.

Is it that your advisor doesn't know or they just don't care?

CHAPTER 9:
SECRETS REVEALED

Today people over the age of 55 face economic conditions much different than previous American retirees. The media attempts to make parallels to past decades, but this situation is different – much different. I want to make sure that I explain to retirees (and those soon to be retired) important facts like the true impact of investment risk. I want to be sure that folks over the age of 55 understand the return needed after a loss just to get back to even. This math is simple, yet rarely discussed. As we age, the amount of time required to recapture our losses with the large gains needed becomes very difficult. It may take years of gains just to get back to where we started *(see exercise and chart on page 51)*. A lot of us fear being embarrassed by our lack of investment knowledge and we just blindly trust an advisor. The question is, do you truly have an advisor to guide you through the turbulent times, or are you in the hands of a financial salesperson with motives tied to his or her own best interests, not yours? Tom Brokaw called your age group "the greatest generation" for a reason. You worked, you saved, you raised your family, you sacrificed and went without to accumulate the money you now have for your retirement and eventually for your family. To place blind faith in a financial system that no longer can hide its flaws is hazardous. Please have the courage to do something positive about it. By the way, I don't mean to sound like an alarmist. Nor do I want to profess that I possess all the answers (no one does). I simply want to encourage you – and others – in a way that no other broker, banker, advisor, lawyer or accountant could ever do. Frankly, I'm a little reluctant to mention that many advisors are in fact financial salesmen and not advisors at all. But, my colleagues persuaded me to explain the truth about how the money system in our country really works, so that you can find the courage to take action. Anyway, this really shouldn't be about me at all. It's all about you, your life with your family and sense of security.

Way back when, we all thought getting a better value for our money meant buying the CD at the bank with the highest rate and Estate planning meant having a will. Things have come a long way since then. Although the economy is turbulent and the government has gone wild with our money, opportunity still exists. It takes courage to face up to things like volatile markets, fast-talking financial salespeople, long-term care concerns and Wall Street money traps. It might seem easier to ignore it or deny it, or to just hold on, tough it out and see where it all goes. But I honestly believe you and your family deserve better.

If you're worried, unsure, unhappy, or losing sleep about what your money, your retirement and your financial future will be, then do something about it. Pick up the phone and call me!

SOUND FAMILIAR?

If you invested $100,000 into a mutual fund that experienced a 20% loss, you would lose $20,000. The account value on your next statement would be $80,000.

Question: For you to get your statement balance back to $100,000, will a 20% gain recoup your loss?

Let's crunch the numbers:
$80,000 x 20% = $16,000
$80,000 (beginning balance)
+ 16,000
$96,000

Answer: No, a 20% loss followed by a 20% gain does not get you your principal back. In fact, to regain your original principal balance you will need to get a 25% return.

REQUIRED RETURN TO REGAIN YOUR PRINCIPAL

% LOST	% GAIN NEEDED
20%	25%
30%	42.85%
40%	66.7%
50%	100%

Your Right Advice Giver
Step 1: Don't go it alone!

The rules of the game are changing rapidly today. You need trusted guides who focus on solving these types of financial and legal problems. These trusted guides won't be found in the form of your favorite bank teller, nor at the local coffee shop, beauty salon or golf course. The greatest protection available will be with specialized professionals.

Step 2: If it sounds too good to be true, it probably is.

It's a common and scary trend today to hear about seniors who have made poor decisions based on "buying into great opportunities." For instance, if a financial salesperson tells you about a 9% CD when you know darn well the bank down the road is paying 1.25% on CDs, guess what? That's a red flag – a giant, waving red flag. When you hear something that sounds good and you want to believe it, ask the person this simple question: "So, what are the strings attached?" If they say "no strings," then you need to turn and run. There are a lot of great financial products with attractive features. But even the great opportunities out there come with "rules" (aka "strings attached"). You need to know what they are and if they are acceptable to you and in line with your planning goals. Always use and trust your own good judgment and common sense.

Step 3: Beware of "free." There is no free lunch.

Marketers use bait-and switch techniques on retirees constantly. Let me outline a few that we are very wary of. First, let's dissect the free lunch or dinner seminar offer. Obviously, when you get an invitation saying, hey I'll buy you dinner – no worries, nothing is ever sold, your good old common sense should kick in and say, "This person is going to do something to get my money." Red flag. I'm certainly not saying you shouldn't go to seminars to learn. We do monthly seminars, but our newspaper insert invites people to come and *learn,* not to eat a free steak dinner. Also be careful of organizations that say they help veterans get benefits for "free." In reality, these are financial salesmen. You can only get help with VA matters from a veteran service organization (like the VFW), an accredited agent or a certified lawyer. Again, "free" here ends up costing you money.

Step 4: Watch out for legal advice from non-lawyers.

We know the value of integrating specific financial products into your estate plan. However, be very cautious when the purchase of a financial product also entitles you to free legal documents to support the plan. This is where you can be penny-wise and fortune-foolish. Our business model is designed for collaboration among like-minded professionals focused on meeting the goals and objectives of the client. No one professional can wear all of these hats and be good at all of these jobs. A key defense from a suffering financial plan is to realize legal documents cost money; and a packaged offer with legal documentation included (based on the purchase of a product) should be a giant red flag.

Step 5: Beware of online "resources."

Information online should be viewed with a very skeptical eye. Today it is not uncommon for retirees to jump online to do "research." The critical question is, are you getting information from a credible source? This can be very difficult to decipher online. Information overload is another problem. If you enter the keyword "safe investments" on Google, you'll come up with about 962,000 articles, websites and "resources" to look at. The problem is, before you finished looking at 962,000 online "resources," you'd be dead and your family would be burdened by the cost and time delay of probate! (Obviously this would defeat your original planning goal.) Yes, you need to do research, but on the right thing – *finding the right help.* Focus your due diligence on finding the right planning team to assist you (as we discussed in step one).

Step 6: Demand proof!

There's nothing worse than getting sold a bad idea. Slick talk can be very persuasive, but it may prove financially disastrous. When seeking professional advice, we recommend that you assess just how accomplished your potential advice-giver really is. How that person answers the following questions should give you a good idea of their qualifications and passion for their work.

- *Are you an author on this subject?*
  Professionals who take time to write have a passion for what they do. They've taken time to spell out their planning methods and beliefs. It's not easy writing a book, so they are dedicated and serious about their profession and proud of what they do. Plus, you'll be able to obtain their book, read it and then check that the advice that they are giving you is in line with the message they published in their book.
- *Do you invest in your professional knowledge?*
  This question is a great way to gauge the prospective advisor's commitment to staying current on new laws, tax code changes and cutting edge ideas to help preserve and grow your wealth. Same goes for financial advisors. If you have a large IRA, you might be swayed knowing an advisor has trained with Ed Slott, a recognized expert CPA in the area of IRA planning. Likewise, an advisor who invests nearly $24,000 a year to belong to an elite advisor coaching group is certainly educated on the latest and most effective investment planning strategies available to preserve and protect their clients' life savings.
- *Which professionals refer business to you?*
  It's common to ask for references, but I believe this is a loaded proposition. It wouldn't be too hard to find three or four people who like an advisor or lawyer and would give them a good reference. Our question is much different. That certainly means more than just having a friend or client say nice things about us. The professional referral source has zero incentive to give false praise. To them it's all about how well we get the job done. This is a much more credible source of information to assess just how good an advisor or lawyer is at

their craft. Again, truly effective planning advice comes from well-organized teams of professionals, which is logical since no one person can be good at all things.

Step 7: Be smart and trust your feelings.

Much is revealed when you meet face to face. See how you feel. I believe that every person who walks through my doors needs to be treated as if they are a member of my own family. I invite you to come meet me and my team, see if you feel comfortable and more secure about your future. There's no cost or obligation to become a client and/or to understand which options are best for you and your family.

UNTIL WE MEET AGAIN

I hope this book opened your eyes and expanded your mind, as that is my ultimate goal. Think about what you have learned. I want you to stop and take inventory of what you're doing, and ask the questions: "Does my advisor *really* understand the true dynamics of securing my retirement dreams? Are they doing the best thing for me?"

With the right planning, you too can have a financially secure, successful retirement. Like the climber who scales Mt. Everest or the vacationer attempting to navigate the rapids, you need an educated advisor who wants to do what's best for you and your loved ones...... Not someone who is simply motivated by sales percentages. It's up to *you*. If you do not work with somebody who understands the concepts outlined in this book, you might need to make a change.

Now that you have the knowledge; there are no excuses!

Is it that your advisor doesn't know, or they just don't care?

What are you going to do about it?!

Made in the USA
Charleston, SC
27 March 2012